He Knows You

Written by Jill S. Lash

Illustrated by Shari Darley Griffiths
and Heidi Darley

ISBN 13: 978-1-4621-3932-3

Published by CFI, an imprint of Cedar Fort, Inc.
2373 W. 700 S., Springville, UT 84663
Distributed by Cedar Fort, Inc., www.cedarfort.com

The library of congress has cataloged the previous edition as follows:

Lash, Jill (Jill Snow), 1984-
He knows you / written by Jill Lash ; illustrated by Shari Griffiths and Heidi Darley.
p. cm.
Summary: God knows when we are feeling down, or happy, or need help apologizing, or when we are scared, but most importantly, he wants us to know that he loves us no matter how we feel.
ISBN 978-1-59955-089-3
1. God--Omniscience--Juvenile literature. 2. Identification (Religion)--Juvenile literature. I. Griffiths, Shari. II. Darley, Heidi. III. Title.

BT107.L37 2010
231'.4--dc22

2009043218

Jacket and book design by Megan Whittier
Edited by Megan Welton

Printed on acid-free paper

Printed in the United States

10 9 8 7 6 5 4 3 2 1

Dedication

To my loving husband, Brad,
and the children I hope to read this story to one day.

We are all children of our Heavenly Father. We lived with Him in heaven before we came to earth. He knows and loves each one of us, including you.

He knows when you are happy.

He knows when you need His help apologizing.

He knows when you are frightened.

He knows when you are feeling down and need to be cheered up.

He knows when you need help telling the truth.

DO NOT
EAT!

He knows when your feelings are hurt.

He knows when you are feeling lonely.

He knows when you pray to Him.

He knows when you do good things.

He knows when you choose the right.

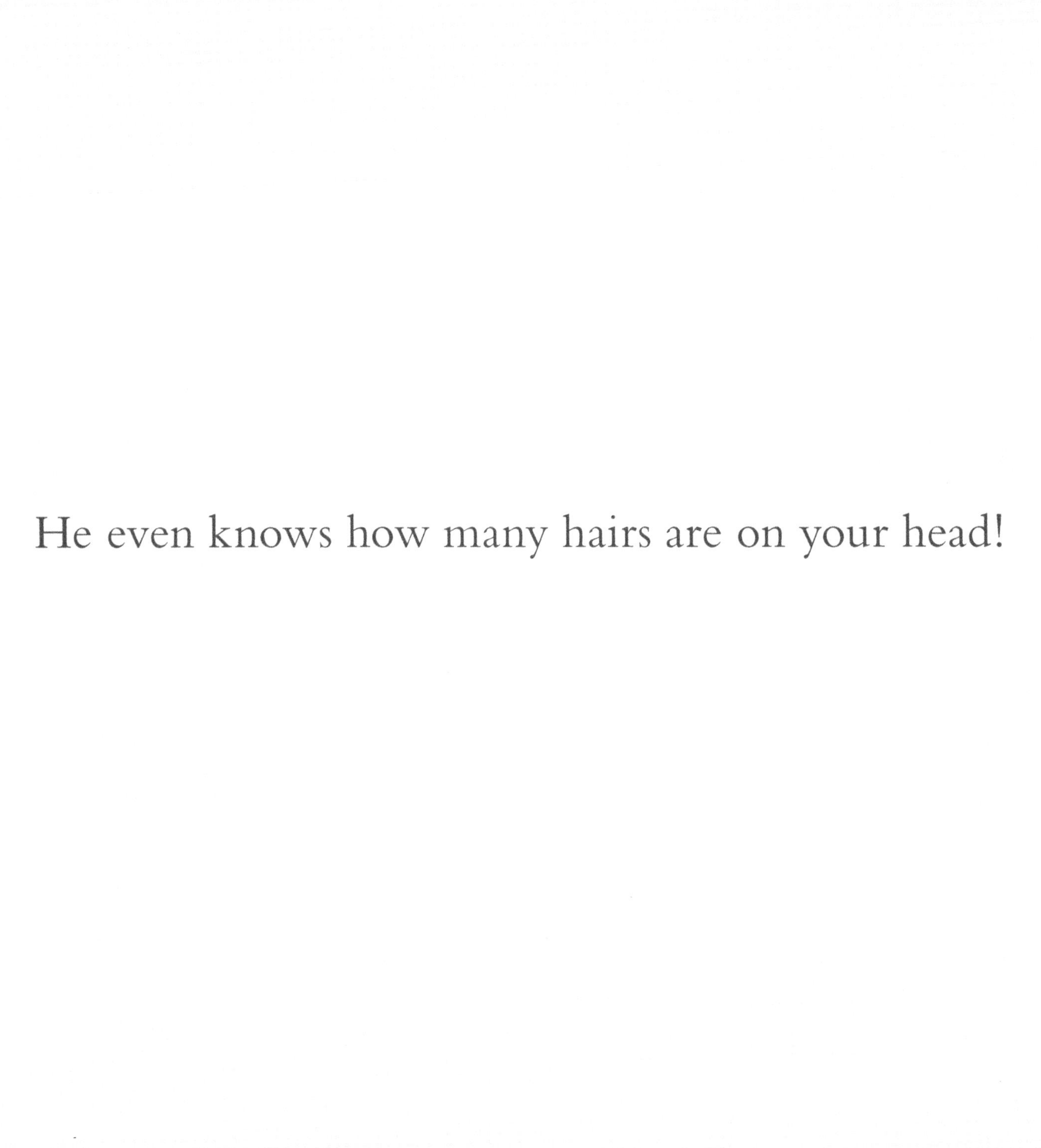

He even knows how many hairs are on your head!

He knows that you love Him.

But most important, Heavenly Father wants you to know that He loves you too.

HOLY BIBLE

HE KNOWS YOU.